# Toaster Haiku

Written and Illustrated by Haley McAndrews

A big welcome to
My first book of poetry;
Come meet my toasters!

This book of poetry is dedicated to my stepsons,
Connor and Joel, who told me I shouldn't write it.
I still love you. – HM

Written and Illustrated by Haley McAndrews
Font: Theano Old Style Regular by Alexey Kryukov
Illustrations: Pen and ink on paper
This is a work of fiction. Any resemblance to actual events or persons,
living or dead, is entirely coincidental.

Published by Red Stone Art Studio.
First paperback edition April 2024, printed in the United States

ISBN 979-8-9851303-4-8 (paperback)
ISBN 979-8-9851303-5-5 (ebook)

www.RedStoneArtStudio.com

## AUTHOR'S NOTE

Haiku is a form of Japanese poetry, introduced to America
somewhere around the year 1900. Each poem has a total of
17 syllables and consists of three lines:
5 syllables in the first line,
7 syllables in the second,
and 5 syllables in the third line.

When I was in 6th grade, I was given an assignment to write
five poems. I wrote over thirty haiku that evening.
The short length and set syllabic structure just make sense to me.

Traditional haiku are written about nature, but you'll find
very little of that in this collection. Instead, I mixed my
playful toasters with text and simple ink illustrations
and baked it in a haiku-shaped dish. While I know my toasters
aren't everyone's cup of tea (or should I say slice of bread?)
I sincerely hope you enjoy my Toaster Haiku.

Haley McAndrews

Five, seven, and five:
All seventeen syllables.
So many toasters!

Wires, cords, hot dry bread,
Gleaming chrome, and crumb tray too.
Kitchen essential.

Rise like toasted bread!
Time to get up for the day.
A morning jump start!

A noble toaster,
With bravery, it goes forth.
But first, eat breakfast!

Not a toaster, but
What about a blender or
Stove? Wrong book, my friend.

In the toaster world
Fork trees grow, lion sun shines
And turtle moon glows.

What are their feet for?
Freedom: running in the wild!
Don't scorch the counter.

Playing in the leaves,
They love to run; race around.
Silverware forest.

Just over the ledge,
Looking out the front window:
Little toasters' view.

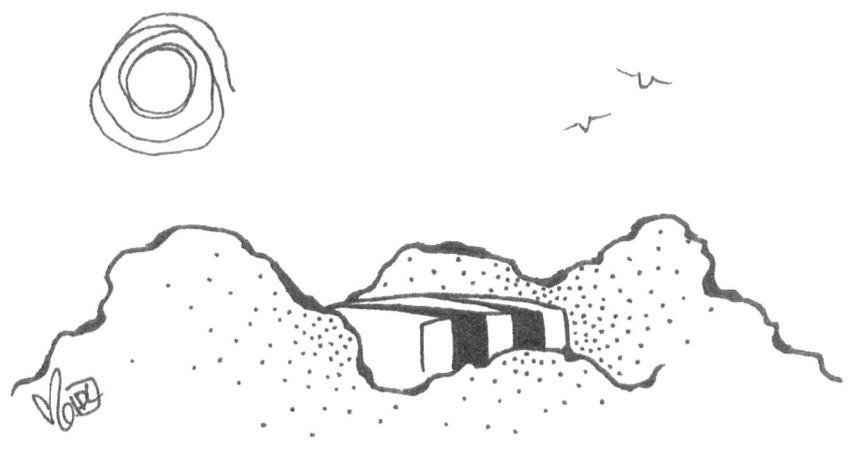

Warm day. Toaster will
Dig a hole in the sandbox!
Sand in the crumb tray.

A trip to the lake!
No fish were found here today,
Just soggy circuits.

Do they eat the bread?
They have no mouth to eat with.
I will eat the toast!

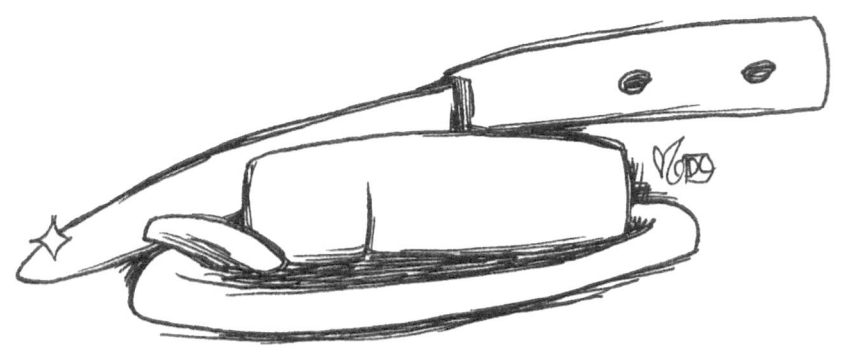

Setting two-point-five.
The perfect amount of heat!
Pass me the butter.

A mid-winter storm;
Travel only with caution.
White toaster gets lost.

Playing in the snow,
They generate their own heat:
Melted snow-toaster.

One by one in line,
A parade of my toasters.
Celebration toast!

Toasters in the store.
See the whole appliance aisle.
Adopt a toaster.

18

Such variety:
So many colors for all
What a fancy style!

I may be obsessed.
My husband does not approve.
I still draw toasters.

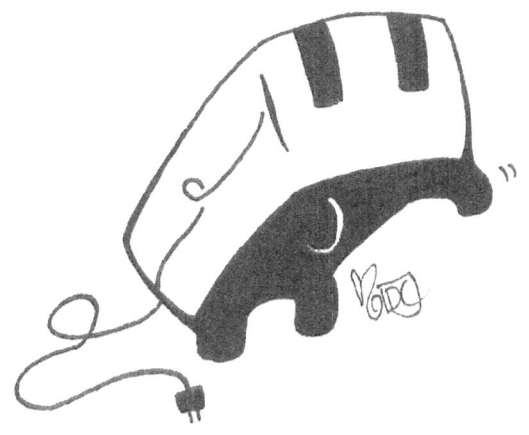

People ask: "Toasters?"
It *is* pretty weird, I know.
Embrace the toasters.

Wow! A bread dryer.
Why do they captivate us?
Inexplicable.

Personally I
Prefer a bagel to toast.
Toaster doesn't care.

What's that? Alarm sounds!
Smoke billows; the toaster stinks.
Oh no! Burnt the toast.

Left side runs too hot!
Many years and sentiments...
I will eat black toast.

Oh, dirty crumb tray.
I know you need maintenance,
But who has the time?

No need for a brush
Hair is a fire hazard.
Maybe use for crumbs?

Up on the counter
Delicious, but out of reach!
It wants the cookies.

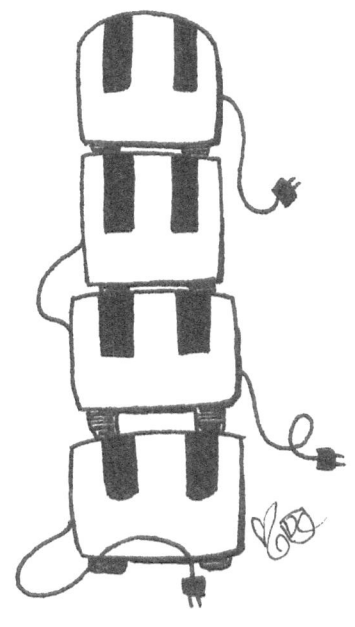

Stacking the toasters
No need for building blocks here!
A toaster tower.

A 4-slice model:
Just as wide but so, so long.
A Dachshund toaster.

A tiny oven.
A mammoth of a toaster.
The toaster oven.

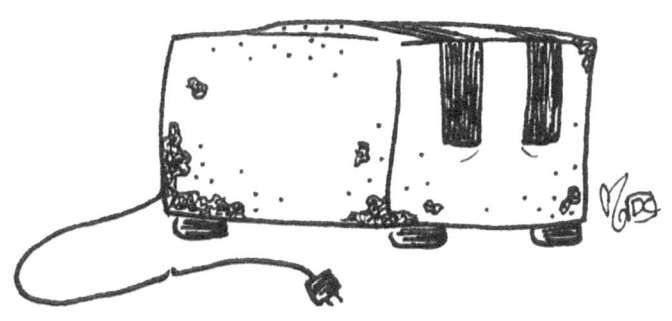

Corners start to rust,
Time doesn't wait for toasters.
Unfit for toasting.

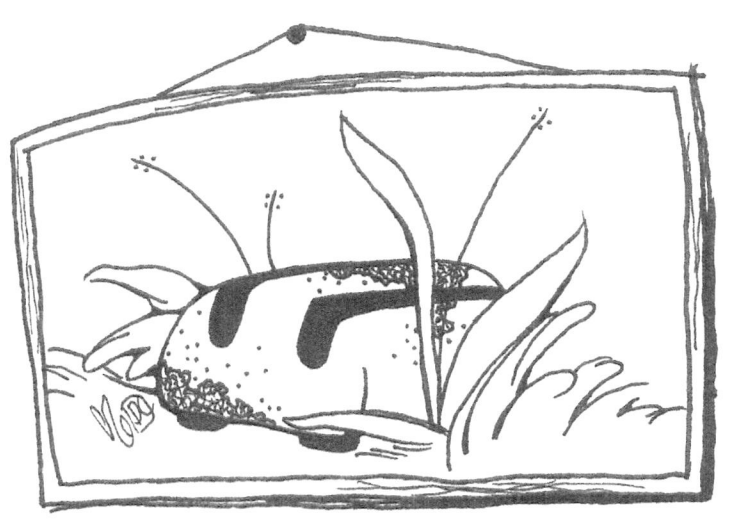

The rust grows, untamed.
Formerly chrome, now turns brown.
Now it is decor.

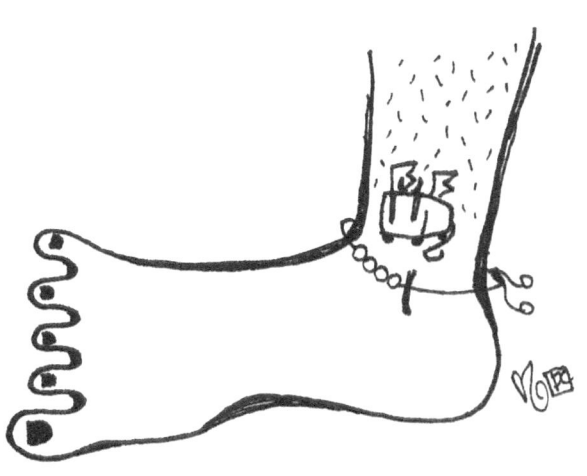

I will admit that
I have one on my ankle.
Toaster self-portrait.

Snuggle in pillows.
Time to say goodnight, toaster.
Snug and toasty dreams.

Here we are, The End.
Toasters love you, send you hugs.
See you next time, Friend!

# Fun Facts

"Why toasters?" they ask.
"The people want toasters, so...
I make more toasters."

The words "toaster" and "toasters" occur
39 times in this book.
There are 67 toasters drawn in this book.
There are 38 haiku poems in this book.
There are only 2 pages in this book without a poem.

www.ingramcontent.com/pod-product-compliance
Lightning Source LLC
Chambersburg PA
CBHW021005150626
46549CB00012BA/1338